at home with color

at home with color

matthew & grainne dennison *photography by* chris everard

RYLAND
PETERS
& SMALL

LONDON NEW YORK

ISBN-10: 1-84597-148-5
ISBN-13: 978-1-84597-148-9

Library of Congress Cataloging-in-Publication Data

Dennison, Matthew.
  At home with color / Matthew & Grainne Dennison ;
photography by Chris Everard.
      p. cm.
  Includes index.
  ISBN-13: 978-1-84597-148-9
  1. Color in interior decoration. I. Dennison, Grainne. II. Title.
NK2115.5.C6D46 2006
747'.94--dc22

                            2005029953

Printed in China

First published in the United States in 2006
by Ryland Peters & Small
519 Broadway, 5th Floor
New York, NY 10012
Text copyright © Matthew and Grainne
Dennison 2006
Design and photographs copyright
© Ryland Peters & Small 2006

10 9 8 7 6 5 4 3 2 1

Senior editor
Clare Double

Location research
Tracy Ogino

Production
Paul Harding

Art director
Anne-Marie Bulat

Publishing director
Alison Starling

Editorial director
Julia Charles

contents

introduction

You could be forgiven for feeling there is a conspiracy. Modern architects, realtors, and even a number of interior designers unite in eschewing the use of color in interiors. Open a newspaper or magazine, look at a realtor's particulars, and the vision that greets you is probably overwhelmingly neutral, if not completely white. Why?

Color is exciting, inviting, stylish, and modern. In a handsomely proportioned 19th-century London house, bold, vibrant colors create an instant sense of welcome and drama. Bright pink and oily Prussian blue appear assertively of-the-moment, reclaiming the grandeur of the architectural context for informal 21st-century family life. Extensive use of white balances the richness of these colors. White-painted architectural elements such as the cornice, baseboards, and door frames "contain" the vivid color, preventing it from overwhelming the space. Strong colors are daringly combined: a glossy orange lampshade sings out against blue walls, a Brunswick green armchair sits on an amethyst rug. In this large space, each of the colors has room to breathe. The effect is one of stylish but light-hearted informality, a personal but inviting decorating statement.

The world is getting smaller and, in Western Europe and the United States, decidedly crowded. Space is at a premium. If you can't have more space, fake it. Pretend your house/apartment/loft/cottage is bigger than you know it is by chucking out the chintz, decluttering the clutter, and painting everything white.

They've got a point, of course. Paler colors maximize natural light, which in turn makes rooms feel larger. Reducing the number of objects you've squeezed into a room also increases the impression of space. But what about you? Where in this pale, empty, still-small space is there evidence of your personality, your family, your hopes? What, in such a context, makes you feel at home?

At Home With Color is intended as an antidote to characterless decorating in safe, pale neutrals. It looks at every area of the home and shows how it can be successfully, colorfully decorated. Not all the colors will appeal to everyone. Some are bright, some are very bright. Some are richly saturated, others moodily intense. Some are so pale they're almost white, others so dark they're nearly black. Some rooms *are* white and others black. They're in a variety of locations,

from Norfolk to New York, and range from a tiny "cottage" in London to a canalside apartment in Amsterdam, from family houses to bachelor pads. They embrace myriad colors, styles, and cultural influences. All use color to add comfort, personality, and, most of all, style to every room of the home.

Very few people find themselves in the happy position of living in their perfect home. For some, that perfect home is a cool apartment with floor-to-ceiling windows overlooking a bustling cityscape; for others it's an old cottage with rough plaster walls and stone-flagged floors. Judicious building work can transform any home, however unpromising. But moving walls, raising ceilings, and digging out floors doesn't come cheap and involves considerable upheaval. Color is today's forgotten decorating tool and can transform any space inexpensively and stylishly.

Where there is little light, careful choice of color will make a room vibrant; where ceilings are too high, color can trick the eye into making them appear lower; where rooms are narrow or cramped, the right color maximizes the impact of difficult proportions. Knowing this, of course, can make the prospect of decorating your home even more daunting. Decorating is not just about choosing colors. Every room needs a focus and an internal coherence. Rooms need to work on a practical as well as visual level and must combine comfort and good looks with utility. A room shared with other people needs to feel welcoming at the same time as expressing its owner's personality. Decorating is a vibrant cocktail.

In a New York apartment, walls the color of red pepper skins make maximum use of the cool city light spilling through the window, which is deliberately uncurtained. The window's black-painted frame echoes other black elements such as the pedestal and leather cover of the folding chair, balancing the richness of the wall color. Light is introduced by the subtle gloss of a 20th-century secretary, a brass lamp, and white-mounted drawings. It glints off metal chair legs and the natural sheen of a white goatskin cushion. The effect is of harmony, though individual elements are skillfully mismatched.

Learning how to use color to maximum effect is an important hurdle jumped. Color has a visual and an emotional impact; it affects our state of mind as well as our aesthetic sense. A colored room can excite, embrace, or relax its occupant.

Different colors conjure up different associations, and different rooms of the home fulfill different functions. The successful decorator combines the two so that the color used in a room not only feels appropriate for its space but enhances the way that space works. We have divided this book not by color but by "zone," examining areas of the home individually and showing how the associations and emotional triggers of the color spectrum can reinforce the purpose of each— from cooking to washing, sleeping to welcoming visitors. This is to encourage the decorator not simply to choose a color arbitrarily—though there will always be circumstances when only your favorite color will do—but to think about what a room needs and how you intend that room to work, and then to evaluate how your choice of color can help you realize these aims.

Paints can create almost any effect you want—from adding instant age to a new wall to giving wooden floorboards a gleaming colored glow. Wallpapers are currently available with metallic finishes or flocked with linen, handblocked in the old-fashioned way or screen-printed in zesty patterns. Fabric has not only embraced advances in durability and color resistance but looked again at old ideas: you can buy cushions made of paper, or glove-soft suede die-stamped like broderie anglaise for handsome modern curtains. Paint, wallpaper, fabric, flooring, furniture, lighting, and decorative accessories have a role to play in every home. In the colored home that role is exciting and infinitely varied.

ABOVE **This deliberately dark scheme shows how comfort can be achieved through texture. Natural materials— wood, leather, and stone—are richly colored and each has its own sheen, catching and reflecting light despite the darkness of the colors. The effect is cocoon-like, a room that is comfortable and inviting despite the scarcity of decorative objects or fabric elements.**

RIGHT **In an Amsterdam apartment, one wall of the home office/dining room is painted with blackboard paint, its soft surface echoed by the dark floorboards. Against the wall, an idiosyncratic book "shelf" has the impact of an art installation. The black background allows the books to function as colorful mini artworks. The varnished floorboards reflect the light, as do quirky Plexiglas chairs and the metal-clad table, illustrating the way texture and material can be used to inject light into a dark-colored room.**

welcome with color

First impressions count. Like it or not, it is worth bearing in mind this simple truism when decorating your home. The appearance and atmosphere of the entrance to your home will affect you and everyone who visits you every time you or they enter the front door. For your own happiness, an entrance hall needs to be more than a sterile transitional space en route to the main living areas. For the benefit of your friends and visitors, it needs to create a sense of warmth and welcome.

No single element overwhelms this boldly colored scheme for the entrance hall of an apartment in New York decorated by Jamie Drake. Vivid pink walls ground a collection of multicolored-stripe paintings and echo the glossy surface of the circular table. Architectural details such as the window frame are painted the same intense pink as the walls.

Until the 16th century, people really knew about halls. Known as the Great Hall, this was the room in which families ate, entertained, and lived. It had the largest fire in the house and the richest decoration. Here, in this single room, quantities of people were entertained. Only as the century progressed did families retreat into smaller chambers discrete from the Great Hall and the entrance hall as we know it come into being. In the 17th and early 18th centuries, hall walls were painted to look like stone. So completely had halls ceased to function as a room that they were seen simply as an extension of the exterior, a halfway house, hardly part of the interior at all. By the middle of the 18th century this was beginning to change and the hall we know now came into being.

For many people today hallways are small, with limited natural light. It's easy to forget that this "in-between" space is a room

and, what's more, the one room that everyone who visits you will see. It deserves attention. It should be recognizably an extension of your personality and your decorating style. Equally importantly, it needs to offer a sense of greeting to friends and visitors—and to you. A hall should say, "This is home" and, more than that, "This is *my* home." Entrance halls should embrace, not intimidate.

In town houses, cottages, or apartments, there may not be space for comfortable furniture or the decorating props we take for granted. In such cases, a finite number of elements have to provide the sense of comfort usually created by upholstery and plump cushions, curtains, or a handsome picture. If you choose your colors carefully, you can create an instant illusion of warmth in keeping with the style of your home.

As with any room, the style options are many and varied. Don't automatically assume that a small, badly lit hall needs an off-white palette and minimal furnishings: it's a short step from fashionable taupe to seventies magnolia, and it is one best left untrod. In the same way, a large hall is not a reason to explode all your fireworks in a single burst. Hold something in reserve for the rest of the house.

If the hall is small and light levels poor, don't run shy of strong color. Harness the positive associations of vibrant colors to create an

In a tall London town house, decoration of the staircase— rising through several floors— changes gear halfway. The main first-floor corridor (OPPOSITE) **is painted an intense, bubblegum pink, balanced by white baseboards and neutral flooring. A pair of acid green- covered side chairs has also been painted white, and black-** **and-white photographs are simply framed with deep white mounts. At landing level** (ABOVE)**, pink walls give way to white, and the neutral flooring is replaced by a boldly striped runner laid over white-painted stairs. The banisters are also white and the walls are bare of pictures, giving prominence to the colorful runner.**

White floorboards harmonize with soft lilac walls in the hall of a family house in the country (OPPOSITE)**; the scarlet wall of a rear corridor draws the eye. On a steep London staircase** (RIGHT)**, scarlet carpet sings out against a neutral background of black walls, banisters, and window frame. Glossy scarlet also provides the answer for a boxy coat closet in a town-house entrance hall** (BELOW)**.**

atmosphere that is uplifting and not too serious, an antidote to possibly cheerless weather outside. Establish your decorating credo right away: be bold and brave at the outset. A colorful entrance is a welcoming one, whether the colors used are inspired by nature on the other side of the front door, a favorite picture, or the need to inject light into a difficult, dark corridor. Avoid the timid option of choosing

> **A colorful entrance is a welcoming one, whether the colors used are inspired by nature on the other side of the front door, a favorite picture, or the need to inject light into a difficult, dark corridor.**

Both these hallways lack a direct source of natural light. In each case, clever use of color makes up the shortfall. A wall of translucent, colored-glass panels within a green-painted frame creates a bright checkerboard (LEFT). **A red-painted chair provides a note of contrast. In a large hall in Provence** (RIGHT), **rich Pompeiian-orange walls echo the earthy note of the stone-flagged floor and the gilded details of the muscular console table, the heavily carved picture frame, and the sunburst mirror. The simple black-and-white drawing and coral and shell ornaments balance the richness of the scheme.**

something bland. The right shade of yellow is exciting and dramatic; water it down and it's anemic and enervating. Since for many people a hallway is effectively little more than a corridor lined with doors terminating in a staircase, steer clear of institutional neutrals or any suggestion of the doctor's waiting room. Remember, too, that your hall is a principal artery of your home; it does not stand alone and, when choosing colors, it is crucial to avoid jarring notes.

Be open to suggestions. Lime green, fuchsia pink, and intense orange can look just as modern as white. In finishes with a sheen or gloss and carefully lit, they will also reflect just as much light into a room. In a city apartment, paired with a simple decorative treatment, these saturated colors provide a promise of a stylish, trendy, modern home. In older houses in town or country, they bring out the high gloss of antique mahogany, the soft glow of well-worn flagstones and the subtle gilding of a carved picture frame. Color has no stylistic allegiances; it can work in any context for owners of all ages and tastes. A tiny vestibule too small to hang a coat in becomes an 18th-century library painted rich turquoise and hung with green-mounted black-and-white engravings. Dark green and deep red, traditionally used in Victorian houses, are reborn for the present day

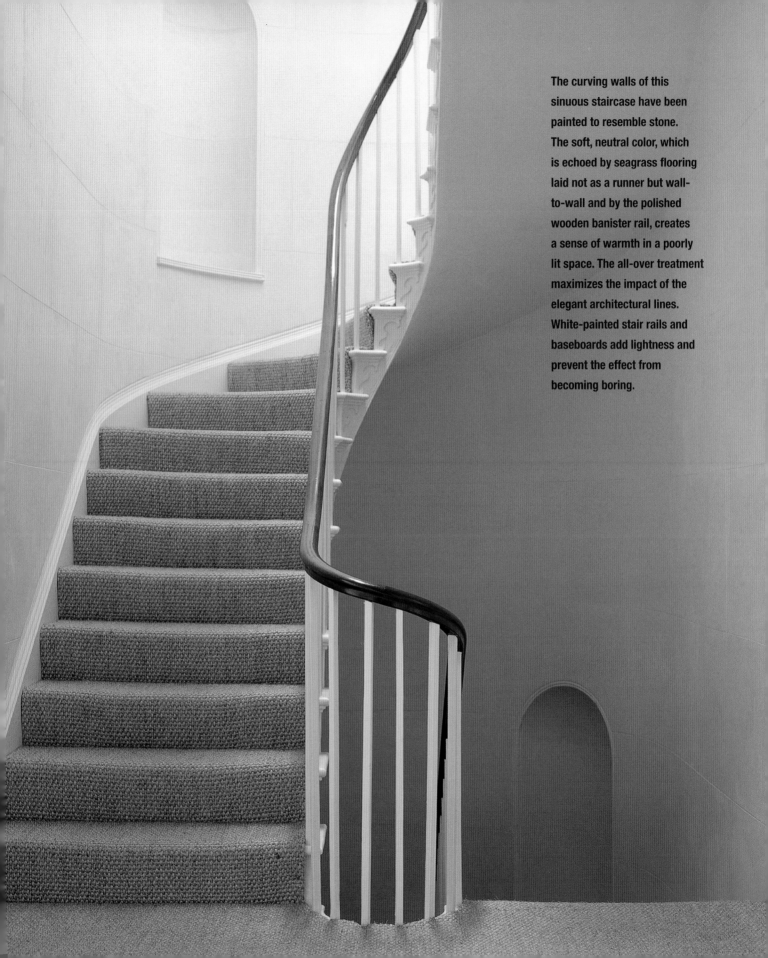

The curving walls of this sinuous staircase have been painted to resemble stone. The soft, neutral color, which is echoed by seagrass flooring laid not as a runner but wall-to-wall and by the polished wooden banister rail, creates a sense of warmth in a poorly lit space. The all-over treatment maximizes the impact of the elegant architectural lines. White-painted stair rails and baseboards add lightness and prevent the effect from becoming boring.

with white woodwork to let in the light. Alternatively, use soft blue and chalky pink to create an informal, contemporary atmosphere. If your instinct is to go pale, paint the ceiling and woodwork white, then think again. Accents of white balance more colorful notes and prevent the color from overwhelming the space. Remember that you are unlikely to spend long periods of time in the hall, so it is safe to opt for something a bit daring here. Corridors and passages can be architecturally boring: bold color adds life and energy to such spaces.

welcome with color

In the past, owners of grand country houses used their halls as showcases for their travels, furnishing them with sculptures and paintings. Today, many of us have been inspired by something we saw on vacation. You may not have room to house a full-size statue of Venus in your hall, but lacquering the walls bright pink—the navy blue of India—and hanging a funky ethnic mirror or colorful Moroccan lantern instantly recalls your travels. You may have spent childhood family vacations in New England or in Cornwall, England. Pale-painted tongue-and-groove boarding, especially when paired with a painted floor, suggests New England, Scandinavian, and English seaside influences, creating a vacation feeling that lasts all year. In a hall, affixing tongue-and-groove paneling to the lower part of the walls also protects them from the knocks of shopping bags, bicycles, and umbrellas. Walls paint-effected burnt umber or deep sienna red capture the magic of Italy—if properly handled, more crumbling palazzo than local pizzeria.

FAR LEFT **Walls with white-painted dado rails mean that this Nile-green staircase remains light and pretty. A striped stair runner in complementary colors cleverly directs the eye through an open door to a wall of pictures.**

LEFT **This 18th-century staircase uses several shades of gray-green in a way that is tranquil and unassertive, and contrasts with the warmer colors of the room beyond.**

A combination of the bold, predominantly green artwork, the materials—polished pine floorboards and a light-reflecting Plexiglas chair— and careful lighting provide the color in this London hallway. The space incorporates a home office and even a microwave.

Unless your hall fulfills a double role (serving as a dining room at night, for example), it is likely to be fairly sparsely furnished. Attention is focused on the limited quantity of furniture and, inevitably, on the walls and floor. Architectural woodwork also acquires greater prominence in such a relatively empty space and can be used as a means of introducing color. Don't overlook doors, baseboards, window frames, and cornices. John Fowler, the doyen of traditional English decorating, frequently painted baseboards black or dark gray to stunning effect. Avoiding white baseboards and cornices can reduce the boxy feeling in a hall, while painting the baseboards the same color as the walls stretches the walls and intensifies your color hit. It can also help you to use bold colors successfully, as the absence of any white counterfoil removes the element of stark contrast, a technique seen in both historic houses and very modern interiors. Try experimenting with a combination of colors: biscuit with yellow, gray and silver with pink, or the muddy grays and browns of 18th-century paint scrapes with paler walls.

At the end of the same hall, two complementary neutral colors have been used for the end and side walls to balance the rich, caramel sheen of the wooden floor. Neutral accessories—the gunmetal tripod lamp and small circular wall clocks—maintain the understated feeling. Roses in a simple cylindrical vase add changing accents of color.

Think of the rooms that lie off the hall. In an apartment, every room may open off the same central space: the decoration you choose needs to work with your kitchen, living room, bedroom, and bathroom. In most houses, bedrooms are upstairs. In a town house, the entrance hall may only lead to the kitchen and the staircase, which leaves your options much more open. But remember that this is your chance to shape first impressions. Don't waste that chance—or the chance to create an uplifting, interesting space you will see every day. Take a deep breath and be bold. Your hall is the first step to creating your perfect home.

no-color color

A pale hall is tranquil and restful, and does not detract from the bolder decorative effects employed elsewhere in the house. But it can also appear joyless, particularly in a town house with limited quantities of murky city light. The no-color hall needs a lift.

Flowers are traditional in hallways. They hark back to earlier ideas of the purpose of this transitional space, embodying the outdoors indoors. They introduce color and a living, natural note, important in a room in which none of us actually lives. There is something in your garden all year round which can be cut for the hall, from the abundant flowers of early summer to knotty stems of evergreens and the spiky silhouettes of dried seedheads in autumn and winter. Like color, there is a flower or stem for every interior—a silver bowl of soft garden roses in the hall of a country house, an Ettore Sottsass vase of purple arum lilies on a Plexiglas console table in a city apartment. City dwellers have the advantage of florists able to locate exotics from Australia or South Africa as well as the earliest Dutch tulips. Country dwellers have hedgerows and the abundance of their gardens. Even a vase of twigs will add color.

Think about the floor. A kilim or Berber runner introduces color without detracting from the overall paleness and allows you to keep walls simple without the effect being boring. Good natural flooring can become a feature in itself and provide the hall's dominant color note. Glossy black slate contrasts with the white walls of a country cottage, wooden floorboards flatter the dairy colors of off-white walls. Designer David Mlinaric frequently uses a muted palette of whites and grays when decorating the halls of historic houses. The effect is elegant and cool, and equally appealing in modern spaces. The gentle background provides a foil for accents of stronger color—in pictures, an exotic light, and, if you're lucky, a window to be curtained in bold fabric.

This monochrome scheme in a New York apartment bravely makes use of only gray, silver, black, and white, creating interest with texture—the scored scraffito effect of the wall treatment; sequins applied to the black-covered footstool; and the vigorously three-dimensional abstract relief hung in a simple, glossy black frame. The textures play games with the light, adding animation to a color-free space.

relaxing with color

In a New York living room, yellow walls and a bright red modular sofa provide a colorful foil to a large, predominantly black-and-white photographic cityscape that dominates one wall. The glossy black floor reflects not only natural light, but also the red glow of the sofa.

We all hanker after the perfect living room, somewhere that makes us feel comfortable and relaxed, delighting the eye with a few carefully chosen decorative objects, a favorite armchair, a photograph in a silver frame, or the much-loved but hideous china animal given to you by one of your children.

The fact is that for most of us the perfect living room never quite happens, our time, energy, and a sizeable chunk of the budget being diverted towards the kitchen, which has become today's alternative living room. Don't despair. The more that most of us live in our kitchens, the more special a beautiful living room becomes. Decorating your living room should be enjoyable: this is a room for family, friends, and fun—and you.

For a lot of people, the living room is the room that requires them to make the largest number of decorating decisions. Decorating a kitchen begins with planning—mapping out cupboards, the placement of appliances, lighting, storage. These technical considerations do not arise in a living room to nearly the same extent, though there are still practical questions to think about at the outset. Where do you put the television, if this is the room in which you intend to watch it? How much seating do you need? Does the room have a fireplace and, if so, are you going to make this the room's focal point? After that, the rule book goes out of the window. It's much harder to decorate a living room that encourages you to relax and feel comfortable than it is to create a functional kitchen, but it can also be much more rewarding. To this end, color is an essential decorating tool. It allows you to express yourself and make your mark on what should be a personal

This large room, which includes two sitting areas, uses vibrant color in a manner that is both disciplined and modern. Only one wall is painted rich tomato red. The color is repeated in striped velvet cushions and balanced by white walls and ceiling, accents of black and furniture upholstered in shades of brown, which are less dominant than the red.

but welcoming space. Background color provides a foil for everything else in the room—from that china animal to the newspapers and magazines that pile up on a footstool in front of the fire, and the Christmas cards that once a year splash their vivid greetings across the mantelpiece.

Remember to be true to yourself. A spirit of common sense informs all the best decorating, however elaborate, and should guide all your decisions. A room only becomes somewhere for you to relax and unwind if it is on the one hand comfortable and on the other decorated in a palette conducive to relaxing. Modern life is fast-paced and demanding. If work means that you spend limited amounts of time at home and even less in your living room, this is still a room that serves a purpose. It is a room for pleasure—somewhere to curl up with a book, the newspaper, or a drink; to watch television, write a letter, or play games with the children; or simply a space in which to sit and chat. Nothing contributes to the desired atmosphere more than the appropriate choice of color (except, possibly, good feather-filled cushion pads on sofas and armchairs).

If in doubt, begin your planning with a mood board. This can be a large piece of cardboard on which you pin pictures of your favorite rooms, furniture, even lampshades, cut from magazines and supplements. Add to it fabric swatches and paint charts, or a postcard of an interior or a painting you particularly like. Taking inspiration from a painting has the advantage that you know that the combination of colors used really works, because you can see the evidence in front of you. Once the board is finished, edit its contents until you're left with a workable combination of colors and textures. Remember to look at the room as a whole. Choosing paint and curtain fabric isn't decorating—your room may not need curtains, perhaps

Black-lacquered furniture and red walls contrast dramatically in this small living room. Seagrass flooring, a blondwood table, polished brass lamp bases, and a chair covered in a red-and-white stripe soften the contrast. Simple nickel shelving and a nickel-colored mirror frame counter the vividness of the red walls, while a ponyskin cushion and leather-covered sofa add comfort and textural interest.

> ❝ **Like all decorating decisions, the use of color needs to be considered as part of the wider equation. In a balanced scheme, no single factor predominates.** ❞

the windows have internal shutters or would be better dressed with wooden blinds than panels of interlined chintz. Consider the floor, the lighting requirements, those extraneous decorative objects such as photographs and vases that accumulate in a living room, all contributing their own color input to the scheme. If you're serious about making your living room somewhere to relax, the chances are it won't often resemble the unnaturally tidy

rooms you've cut out of glossy magazines. Take into account at the planning stage the sort of objects that inevitably come to roost in your living room. There's no point in creating a rigorously disciplined color scheme if the room is going to be home to children's multicolored building blocks or last week's Saturday supplements, or if this is the room in your house where you display any flowers you are given.

Like all your decorating decisions, the use of color needs to be considered as part of the wider equation. In a well-balanced scheme, no single factor should predominate. Ask yourself

a number of questions at the mood-board stage. How do you intend to introduce color to the scheme, and how free a rein do you want to give it? Do you want colored walls; a colored floor or floor covering; a colorful window treatment; colored furniture; colored everything? Do you have a colorful painting for this room and if so, will this inspire the scheme, or will the scheme be intentionally muted as a foil to the artwork? Do you crave a wonderfully colorful modern chandelier or have you bought in a junk store a set of bright antique china plates to display on walls or the chimneypiece? Will you fill this room with flowers or books? Are you starting from scratch with a blank canvas, or do you have to work around the furniture or curtains you brought with you from a previous home? If this is the case and if you want to introduce new colors in addition to those you already have, what is the most effective way of doing so harmoniously? Are you hesitant about using color at all and do you want to restrict it to a few carefully chosen accents? It will be too late to ask these questions once you have filled the room with myriad components.

Historically, living rooms and drawing rooms were a feminine preserve. Women presided over "withdrawing rooms" while their husbands held sway in the masculine surrounds of the library, study, or gun room. Today this

ABOVE **An uncurtained floor-to-ceiling window with white-painted shutters floods with light this warm terracotta-colored country living room, in which the radiator has been painted the color of the walls.**

OPPOSITE **The white background of a modern painting lightens the effect of a rich layering of red on red in this living room-cum-study in a London town house. Accents of black inject contrast.**

distinction has mostly disappeared, but the historical influence persists in two forms: living rooms remain among the prettiest rooms in any home, decorated to be visually appealing to the homeowner and their guests; and they remain partly a public room for entertaining, even if women now share the hostess's role with their partners. Freeing the living room from gender associations has broadened the spectrum of colors commonly used: there are no set rules. As in every room of the house, it's a question of preference married to practical necessity.

> **Different colors conjure up varied associations in our subconscious. Colors can be used to harness happy memories, an important consideration in any room intended to relax its occupant.**

The Georgians and Victorians used color in very different ways. The pale, pretty, fondant shades of late 18th-century interiors by Adam and Wyatt gave way to the burnt umber, porphyry, pink, and turquoise of the Regency, then the richer, darker, more somber hues championed later in the 19th century by Pugin, Crace, and Morris. The decorating revolution of the early 20th century was the fashion for white—white walls, carpets, furniture, and fabrics, as in the famous schemes created by between-the-wars decorator Syrie Maughan. White became the color of modernism since it represented simplicity and a pared-down approach, allowing the lines of a building to be read easily and capitalizing on the effects of natural light within a space. Today white remains the preferred color of modern architects and minimalists.

The modern decorator, however, is not constrained by stylistic allegiances or architectural theories. Many of us live in an old house which we need to work for

A large living room has been given a daring treatment based on a vividly colored wall covering, in which a stylized, Japanese-influenced pattern of flowering branches stands out against a bold, turquoise background. To avoid this becoming overwhelming, the walls are bare of pictures and the black chesterfield sofa has no loose cushions. A decorative brass lamp echoes both the metallic note of the wall covering and its naturally inspired motif.

The carved-pine fireplace wall of this Georgian living room is both decorative and colorful. The remainder of the scheme is built around this focal point. An antique daybed, a pair of mid 20th-century armchairs, and a glass-topped coffee table are made of similarly warm-colored woods, and the palette is kept pale to allow the rich colors of the fireplace wall and the floor to sing out. Pale gray-blue echoes the steely light of the city beyond the window. The cornice has been painted the same color as the walls, which both heightens the walls and makes the ceiling appear cozily lower.

us in a thoroughly modern way. Our possessions include old furniture and new appliances. Even if the pictures on our walls show scenes of the past, the views through our windows are of a modern cityscape or countryside shaped by today's agricultural practices. We prefer a new sofa, with its comfortable stuffing unheard of in the 18th

Book spines are always colorful. In this room in which bookcases are a major feature, the walls have been painted pale, watery blue-green to balance the bright color of the books. A chartreuse chair with a Prussian blue cushion is harmonious and pretty.

> ❝ **Pale, pretty colors show off antique darkwood furniture as effectively as the richer colors of traditional decorating, but give a fresh twist to a room.** ❞

century, but choose an 18th-century dining room table, gleaming with the patina of age. If we crave a Victorian-style claw-footed tub, we want it with state-of-the-art plumbing.

Different colors suggest not only different historical influences but inevitably conjure up varied associations in our subconscious. Colors can be used to harness positive associations and happy memories, an important consideration in any room intended to relax its occupant. Decorating fashions have embraced a similarly open-minded approach, with historically inspired paint ranges remaining as popular as the more recent proliferation of neutral ones, allowing the decorator to choose for himself. What matters is the architecture of a space (it would

be a shame to paint a house by Robert Adam all white or, even worse, taupe), the purpose of the room you are decorating, and the nature, style, and color of the objects with which you intend to furnish that room.

If there is a science behind decorating with color, it is the color wheel. Sir Isaac Newton is credited with identifying the color spectrum in the 17th century. During his time at Cambridge, Newton experimented with prisms. He recorded five colors: red, yellow, green, blue, and violet. Friends persuaded him to add two more, indigo and orange, in order to make a cosmically significant seven. The result is what we now think of as the colors of the rainbow: red, orange, yellow, green, blue, indigo, and violet, imprinted on every British

The brightness of this sky-blue living room has been countered by painting the walls white to dado-rail height. This allows the introduction of additional bright colors, notably the purple armchair. The blue walls flatter a black-and-white drawing and colorful painting.

schoolchild's memory in the mnemonic "Richard of York Gave Battle in Vain."

Today's color wheel is simply a development of Newton's spectrum, and demonstrates the relationship of individual colors within that spectrum. The primary colors of red, yellow, and blue (all of which can't be made by mixing any other colors) are distributed at intervals around the wheel, and divided by the secondary colors green, orange, and violet (made by mixing equal amounts of the primary colors nearest them). Between these six principal divisions are any number of tertiary colors (mixtures of primary and secondary colors), so that the effect as the wheel turns is not of ribbons of distinct color but a gentle progression, the gradual merging of one color into another. The color wheel shows harmonious colors—those that lie

In this London living room, color bridges the gap between Victorian architecture and contemporary furniture. Instead of swags and a gilt-framed mirror above the fire, windows are uncurtained and the mirror frame is white, complementing white furniture and pale floorboards. Inky blue walls contrast with the white and unite the other elements.

next to or close to one another—and complementary ones: markedly different shades that can successfully be used in combination. These lie opposite one another on the color wheel, for example blue and orange. Color wheel complementaries are lively without being jarring and can be used for large- and small-scale inspiration in living rooms, from the color of a sofa to stand on a complementary-colored rug to the color chosen for contrast piping on a slipcover. The wheel is particularly useful for choosing the colors to paint woodwork, cornices, baseboards, and window frames.

In the past, when entertaining and, indeed, domestic life in general were more formal, living rooms were regarded as "important" rooms. In an old house, the chances are the living room will be among the grandest in the house in terms of

plasterwork, cornice, and chimneypiece, and enjoy either the best view or the best light. It may also be one of the largest rooms in the house. Light is the essential factor shaping the effect of the colors you use to decorate, followed closely by volume of space.

If you are choosing paint for a room, paint a large square on each of the walls to be covered and look at the color repeatedly through the course of a day. The effect changes with changing light, from early morning to dusk, in bright sunshine, or the glow of artificial light. It also differs according to position in a room. A patch of wall directly opposite a window, benefiting in full from daylight, will appear a noticeably different color from a patch of wall immediately below a cornice or window sill, behind a door, or on the ceiling. A color you love on a bright, sunny day may not be nearly so appealing when the sky is overcast, or seen by electric light on a winter evening. This is important to bear in mind at the mood-board stage of putting together a scheme and it's important you get it right. Although repainting is an inexpensive way of redecorating if you decide you've made a mistake, it is also inconvenient, requiring the room to be emptied of furniture, curtains taken down, and the floor carefully covered. Nothing can entirely prepare you for the all-over effect of a newly painted room, but by taking this simple precaution, it is possible to steer yourself towards a more accurate idea in advance.

The color wheel won't help you to see how colors work in changing light, but it does at least offer an at-a-glance idea of the character of different colors—their somberness or warmth. A muted tertiary shade including lots of green or blue will need plenty of light if it is to be made cheerful. This may rule it out as your choice

This large room combines the functions of living room and dining room, with a subtle color shift from pink and pale buff at the sitting end (OPPOSITE) **to deeper mauve and amethyst at the dining end** (ABOVE). **In both cases, notes of bold color are balanced by neutral elements: a parchment-colored sofa and simple caramel silk curtains.**

The sitting end of the room shown on the previous page contrasts jewel shades with a neutral backdrop, giving a sophisticated look that is arrestingly colorful but still comfortable. The pink velvet ottoman echoes the circular motif of the large painting so that the eye travels from one to the other. Pink cushions and lampshades create coherence.

what could be a drawback. Used in conjunction with careful lighting, dark colors can even provide the best solutions for small spaces. It's a question of the extent to which you want your chosen color to dominate the finished scheme. It's also worth remembering that a very small space will never appear anything but small whatever colors you use to decorate it. Painting a tiny living room white will make it appear fractionally less tiny, but as soon as you arrange furniture within the space, the illusion is shattered. Rich, opulent colors in the same setting can create the

for a relaxing room you use mostly at night by lamplight. You may also decide that a very bold shade will be too demanding in a smaller room. This is a matter of preference: there are many examples of small rooms successfully decorated in rich, intense colors. The effect is of a cocoon, a womb-like space that can be extremely cozy at night or during colder months. Very strong colors emphasize the enclosed nature of a small space, but do so in a positive manner, making an advantage out of

ABOVE AND RIGHT **A neutral backdrop allows the successful inclusion of several different colors within the same space. In this London living room, lime green, café au lait, and amethyst combine harmoniously. Although the decoration makes use of traditional furniture and accessories, the palette updates the scheme, at the same time creating a comfortable, relaxing atmosphere.**

egg-yolk yellow, Schiaparelli pink, or pale turquoise, all light, bright colors that produce the same effect of richness as intense deep shades, particularly if you choose a paint with a sheen or even glaze or lacquer your walls. Remember that any color that delivers an instant visual "hit" will override all other first impressions of a room. This can be used to your advantage in an oddly shaped room or one that is smaller than you wish, and is particularly useful, for example, in a living room used for cocktail parties, where guests will not look closely but simply take in the overall impression at a glance.

If you are fortunate enough to glory in a well-lit room with good proportions, the world, or rather the color spectrum, is your decorating oyster. How do you see yourself? It's important that your living room reflects that self-perception and feels like *your* room. You *can* be a modern urbanite without resorting to hard edges and white walls:

impression of a jewel box, a room that is exquisite in its smallness. Interior designers often direct clients towards stronger colors than the client would naturally choose. With all of his or her experience, the designer knows that bold and unexpected combinations really work, and is braver than the inexperienced amateur, teaming indigo walls with burnt orange silk, crimson with fudge brown, acid green with violet. If your natural instinct is to be timid but you long for something dramatic, think about painting walls

ABOVE AND OPPOSITE **The painted elements of this living room are pale, but the effect is of warmth and color. Glowing antique mahogany and oak furniture, carefully chosen paintings, and chairs covered in a red-checked tweed add to the sense of comfort and homeyness. Although this room includes a large number of photographs and decorative objects, the effect remains simple and uncluttered, balanced by the pale background.**

OPPOSITE **Charcoal-painted paneling is intensely dramatic and anything but gloomy in this stylish living room, in which dark walls give full prominence to the vibrant painting. The pale marble chimneypiece, green armchair and brass lamp add further accents of rich color.**

ABOVE AND RIGHT **The same color has been used to more modern effect in this sleek scheme in an apartment in Amsterdam. Uncurtained windows flood the space with natural light, while white walls, baseboards, and window frames prevent the dark color from becoming too dominant. A giltwood chair and large-scale damask fabric add decorative interest.**

try pale pink with woodwork in biscuit, charcoal, or even silver. Pastels, reminiscent of a summer's day, soothe and calm, the perfect antidote to harsh city living. A palette inspired by eggshells, pebbles, or the fresh new leaves of spring will bring the prettiness of the country to town. A combination of earth tones can look not only chic but soft and warm; use accents of red for drama and vigor. Take inspiration from French chateaux with chalky greens, yellows, and grays, or use the colors of a summer garden—sweet peas, old roses, delphiniums, and stocks—to create a look that can be traditional, retro, or deliciously girly. Pale, pretty colors show off antique darkwood furniture as effectively as the richer

The graphic modern painting inspired this disciplined scheme in black, maroon, brown, and off-white. Simple furnishings maximize the impact of contrasting textures—unvarnished wooden shutters, velvet cushions on a leather sofa, a piebald goatskin rug.

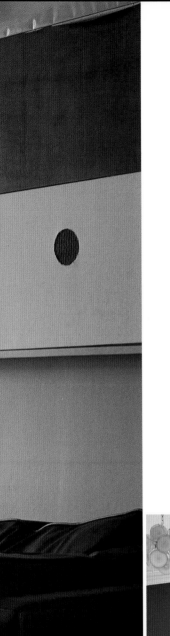

RIGHT **In this living room in New York, the colors of the bold but pretty modern painting are partly echoed in the modular sofa below which, like the painting, wraps around the corner of the room. White and sand-colored cushions provide notes of contrast against blue upholstery. The pink flowers of the painting add warmth to a restrained scheme.**

BELOW **A Victorian living room has been updated with modern furniture and a fresh approach to color: the chimney wall is white, but the remainder of the wall is richly red. A honey-colored modern chandelier breaks up the white ceiling.**

colors of traditional decorating, but give a fresh, modern twist to a room.

The ideal living room makes you feel comfortable and at home. It also exudes the personality of its owner. Frances Partridge, diarist and friend of Virginia Woolf, was delighted when her much-photographed living room in London was described as being the perfect room for a clever person. Painted a strong chalky pink, with elements of green and blue, it had a quintessentially Bloomsbury atmosphere. Spanish pottery, paintings by Dora Carrington and Duncan Grant, and a mosaic by Boris Anrep injected further bold

This white-painted London living room explodes with color. The walls are hung with a vibrant collection of 20th-century flower paintings and a wittily eccentric wall hanging based on the Union Jack. Sofas—one covered in purple velvet, the other with a white slipcover—face one another across a multicolored striped rug, on which a footstool sits, covered in a heavily sequined cloth. Both have bright cushions, several inspired by the paintings' floral motifs.

> **Take inspiration from the colors of a summer garden— sweet peas, old roses, delphiniums, and stocks—to create a look that can be traditional, retro, or deliciously girly.**

color. The effect was elegant, thoughtful, intelligent—adjectives Frances Partidge would have chosen her guests to use.

Think about colors that relax you, about the furniture you own, and those pieces you long for; about favorite paintings, vacation destinations, or clothes. Look at the size and shape of your living room, its windows, and the levels of light. Imagine being in the room on your own, with your husband or wife, with your children, all your family at Christmas, your best friends for a drink after work. And then relax and enjoy your decorating.

The overall impression of this living room is of lightness, despite the honey-colored chenille ottoman, the rich ripe-corn throw over the sofa back, and the early 19th-century daybed upholstered in warm caramel. Against a cool white background, warm neutral shades inspired by the modern painting above the chimneypiece add a sense of comfort as well as visual interest. A Plexiglas coffee table reflects the colors around it and the light from tall windows.

no-color color

A white or neutral living room can accommodate colorful elements without losing its aura of pale restfulness. Instead of curtains in a bold fabric, make cushions and arrange them sparingly on pale sofas. Use vintage fabric for a valance for curtains made from unbleached linen; trim a simple shade with colored ribbon or fringing. Pale schemes need variety as much as their more daring counterparts. Your room may need lamps, vases, cachepots—each can introduce a color note without overwhelming an essentially uncolored room. Instead of paintings, display black-and-white photographs in bright frames, use vivid shades on clear glass lamp bases, stand white sofas on a vibrant kilim. Color will add interest, drama, and luxury to the coolest room.

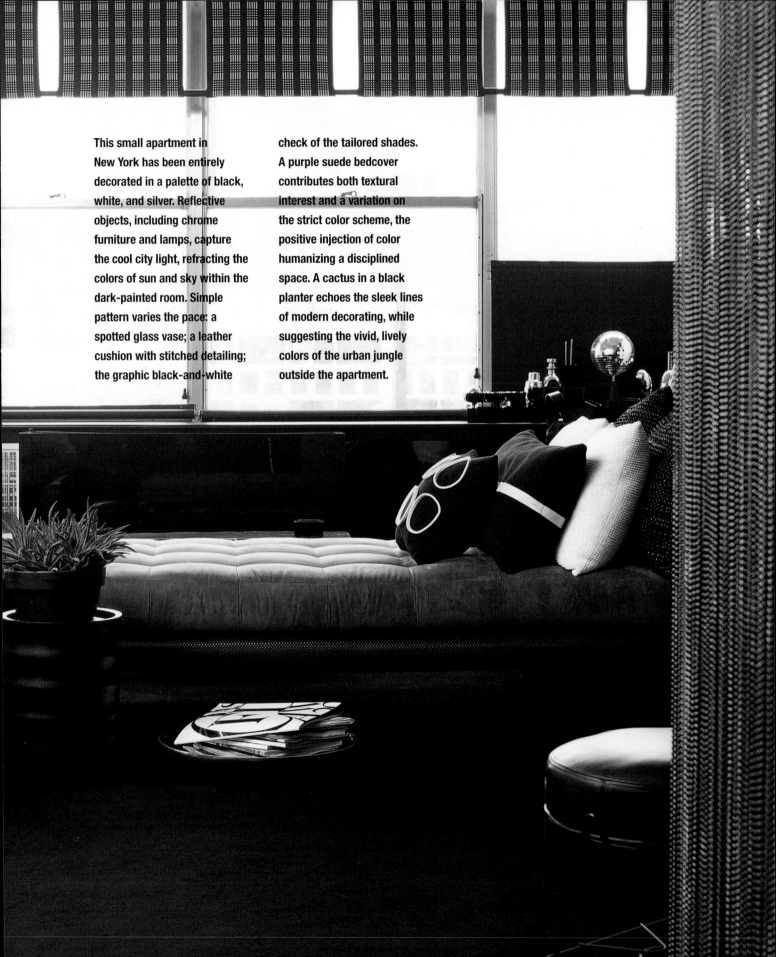

This small apartment in New York has been entirely decorated in a palette of black, white, and silver. Reflective objects, including chrome furniture and lamps, capture the cool city light, refracting the colors of sun and sky within the dark-painted room. Simple pattern varies the pace: a spotted glass vase; a leather cushion with stitched detailing; the graphic black-and-white check of the tailored shades. A purple suede bedcover contributes both textural interest and a variation on the strict color scheme, the positive injection of color humanizing a disciplined space. A cactus in a black planter echoes the sleek lines of modern decorating, while suggesting the vivid, lively colors of the urban jungle outside the apartment.

entertaining
with color

There is no doubt that eating habits have changed dramatically in recent decades; not only what we eat, but where and how we eat meals at home. Kitchen dining has killed the traditional dining room for many people, and smaller modern homes frequently dispense with a dining room altogether.

Hand in hand with eating in the kitchen have come a host of related innovations, chiefly the increasing informality of everyday entertaining and the development of the kitchen as a room in which to live, not simply cook. Kitchen dining is ideally suited to small city apartments, where space is at a premium. It also takes into account the fact that the majority of hosts work during the day. They don't have time to cook in advance of a supper party but begin their food preparation with the arrival of their guests imminent. The trend for guests to congregate in the kitchen with a pre-supper drink allows the cook to see and talk to his or her friends. It also requires a kitchen that is decorated not merely to satisfy the practical requirements of cooking but as somewhere comfortable, good-looking, and atmospheric for entertaining.

For an entertaining space that is attached to or part of your kitchen, the choices you make should take into account the sort of items that will furnish the room, namely kitchen appliances and storage. Do you want a sleek minimalist approach with implements and china concealed from view, or do you prefer to see your china, glass, coffee machine, and toaster? The humble refrigerator has come a

The walls and ceiling of this sleek kitchen are white. Against this background, pale-green lacquered cupboard doors and a simple blue-glass backsplash provide cool injections of color. A part wall features open shelving painted orange, a color traditionally associated with eating rooms, here skillfully updated.

Walls painted rich eggplant purple create instant drama. The color—which would sit well in a traditional dining room—appears stylishly contemporary alongside metal shelving and oak cabinets with simple handles. This is a disciplined scheme, in which the palette is restricted to eggplant and white, with extra color notes provided by wooden cabinets, metal accessories, and herbs.

long way lately. Manufacturers produce models that are as good-looking as they are functional and, rather than concealing your appliances, you may want to decorate around them. A pastel-colored, retro-style fridge, with matching food mixer and toaster, is not something to hide. Be inspired by it to create a sugar-pink kitchen with all the cheery brightness of a fifties diner. Even traditional range ovens are now available enameled in a broad range of colors, with several manufacturers offering a made-to-order coloring service. Remember that whatever appliances you choose, unless you screen them from view, they will all make their own contribution to the appearance of a space, both decoratively and in terms of color. The color decisions you make need to recognize this and aim to create a sense of harmony.

In the past, kitchens were made of painted deal or shiny pine. Happily, those days are gone. Modern kitchens make use of tropical hardwoods such as wenge and iroko, whose rich, dark colors are a far cry from the blond anemia of pine.

> **Of all the rooms in your home, the one you use for eating will lend itself most readily to strong color. Intense, warm colors stimulate the appetite and are closely associated with food.**

All the colors of this elegant dining room are found in the striking painting on the far wall. Complementary shades of pink and purple are balanced by caramel curtains, buff-colored walls and the darkwood chairs. Ormolu-mounted sang de boeuf vases add a note of old-fashioned grandeur—yellow flowers providing contrast—as do the turquoise chandelier pendants.

The boom in designer kitchens means that kitchen cabinets can now be made from just about anything—from painted composite board and Shaker-style cherrywood to brushed steel and vibrantly colored lacquers and laminates (superseding the less versatile Formica). All make positive color statements, not least since, in all but the largest or most minimal kitchens, units and cabinets form the room's biggest component. Your decorating will need to work around these color notes.

For the color wary, one temptation is to opt for banks of sleek white cabinets, which look modern and banish clutter. This may be chic, but it's not ideal for a home with young children, and can look like a laboratory. In such cases, consider softening the look through your window treatment, chair pads or cushions, or by using a tablecloth. The trend for vintage style has spawned a revival in oilcloth, now available in a wealth of pretty and brightly colored designs that could in themselves provide the starting point for a

successful scheme. Introducing color through items such as tablecloths gives you a degree of versatility, since the cloths themselves are so easy to change and allow you to create "dual-aspect" rooms that are warm and child-friendly during the day but sophisticated and grown-up at night. If you plan to vary things in this way, be sure to create a backdrop that will adapt itself to such innovations.

Counters and backsplashes also provide opportunities for introducing color to the kitchen. Counters can be made from any durable heat-resistant material. Reclaimed timber and inky granite offer a modern spin on traditional style. Manmade materials such as Corian, available in a dazzling array of colors from the subtlest off-white to the brightest shocking pink, update the look. Backsplashes—essential behind sinks and stoves—can be made of colored glass to inject a dash of contrasting color. Alternatively, clear glass can be painted on the reverse the same color as surrounding walls for a more discreet,

Color is introduced to this large kitchen in the fuchsia-painted ceiling and dark-stained floorboards. Within this dramatic "envelope," white cabinets reflect light from tall windows. The room is light enough to accommodate a wall of blackboard paint, a surface that absorbs light.

uniform effect. Rethink old-fashioned tiling. Tiles can add color, pattern, or simply a different surface effect to kitchens, from Delft windmills to the distressed metallic sheen of iron ore. Current trends have moved away from traditional motifs in blue and white, but you can still create traditional "country kitchen" color with similar patterns revisited in purple and white or green and white. A checkerboard of plain, colored tiles using two or three colors is bright and modern, as long as you are sure you will not tire of the look. It has the advantage of offering a selection of different colors to echo elsewhere in the scheme, but remember that such a bold statement needs to be carefully balanced. Single-color tiles offer a less assertive color injection.

Appliances, cupboards, and permanent fixtures such as counters and backsplashes, of course, are only the beginning. Color enters a kitchen in many ways, not all of them permanent, including on a plate, in glasses, and in vases. Kitchen storage can take the form of open shelving or glass-fronted cupboards that present to view the china and glassware they house. Traditionally kitchens contained a dresser, used both to store and to show off pretty everyday china, typically rows of blue and white willow-pattern plates. Today the china may be modern—and you may choose white china partnered by richly colored

glass—but visible storage remains an effective way to introduce color to your kitchen.

Kitchen eating and entertaining emphasizes the processes behind the food we eat; it makes few attempts to disguise the business of cooking and carving. This is in keeping with increasing informality in all aspects of domestic life and entertainment, but it doesn't mean that the traditions of yesterday's dining room need be jettisoned entirely. Many eat-in kitchens derive their color from painted walls, and those

LEFT **Part of a corridor has been transformed into an old-fashioned pantry, with deep open shelves for china storage. Shelves, walls, baseboards, and door frames have been painted the same rich green—a positive foil for green and white china.**

RIGHT **In an updated version of the traditional dining room, walls and ceiling have been paint-effected matt terracotta pink. As this is a large room, the expanse of color is broken up by painting the cornice, dado rail, and baseboards off-white.**

walls remain faithful to the traditional dining-room palette of red, green, and orange, colors associated with food and eating regardless of context. The fact that these colors are now used in a room primarily for cooking prevents them from appearing dark, somber, or formal: cooking requires effective task lighting and involves shiny appliances, utensils, and crockery. All balance the richness of traditional dining colors, injecting them with light, pace, and variety. The popularity of kitchen living means that in newly built homes and conversions, the kitchen has superseded the living room as the most important room in the house. New kitchens are often the largest room in the house, restoring something of the grandeur of entertaining, which might have been lost with the demise of the dining room, but doing so in a thoroughly modern way. In the country, the large kitchens of houses built when domestic servants were commonplace lend themselves happily to modern kitchen living.

Of all the rooms in your home, the one you use for eating will lend itself most readily to strong color. This has always been the case. Eating rooms, especially those used at night, have traditionally been richly colored, even in houses in which

the decoration is predominantly neutral. This is partly because intense, warm colors stimulate the appetite and are closely associated with food. Think of the skin of a Seville orange; the glow of old Burgundy; the saturated vermilion reds of tomatoes freshly harvested in a Mediterranean market; the vivid green of new peas; the yellow of pungent saffron or egg yolks. It is also because bright colors provide the ideal foil for the accouterments of traditional dining: pretty china and glass, silver flatware, snowy linen napkins, and candlelight. The silver flatware of the past may have given way to simpler, stainless-steel kitchenware, and mahogany dining room chairs to sleeker models in Plexiglas, polypropylene, and metal, but these still require a carefully chosen background to appear to best effect. The internationalism of today's cooking makes use of exotic ingredients from across the globe,

Both these kitchens use pastels to different effect. In the kitchen on this page, lavender walls combine with wooden cupboards, a shiny metal range stove, and industrial white tiles to soften a chic, modern look. In the kitchen opposite, walls painted the powdery pink of old-fashioned sugar mice are the starting point for a retro look, echoed by the floral shade, Chinese paper lantern, colorful Thermos flasks, and pretty china arranged on the open shelves. In both cases, extensive use of white paint lightens the effect and prevents "feminine" colors from creating overtly feminine schemes.

reinforcing our association of eating with strong color. Fresh inspiration can now be found in the bold skins of tropical fruits, their bright flesh and juices, the warm glow of costly spices, the lustrous sheen of exotic seafood and fish. Remember, too, that warm colors put people at their ease, an important consideration for anyone entertaining.

Unlike dining rooms, kitchens are rooms in which you spend time throughout the day. The rich, dark colors of traditional dining rooms glowed in the gentle light of candles. Any color used in a modern kitchen needs to work daylong, in the first sunshine of the morning and the bright electric light of nighttime. This is a significant factor to bear in mind when planning your scheme, and also applies to dining rooms used chiefly for weekend lunches, when you won't be using candles and need to take advantage of natural light.

Times change but old habits die hard. The Victorians placed such emphasis on flowers for dressing the dining room table that tables were actually cut to accommodate the vessels necessary for extravaganzas of the florist's art. Candlesticks towered above white cloths or gleaming dark wood, catching the facets of intricate cut glass, the deep bowl of a silver spoon, the blue-glass lining of a pretty salt cellar. Flowers and candles remain essential table accessories, though the vases and

ABOVE **At the dining end of this kitchen, a yellow wall provides a flattering backdrop to a large black-and-white cityscape. The picture's matte surface prevents it from dominating; the eye is drawn instead to the reflective metal table pedestal and the sheen of the leather chairs.**

OPPOSITE **Behind open shelving, this wall has also been painted yellow, which throws into relief not only the colored glass and china but also the clear glass, in a way a white wall could not. Against the very dark kitchen cabinets, the injection of color expands the space.**

entertaining with color

This lofty kitchen successfully blends old and new. The sleek lines and neutral colors of the modern kitchen units contrast with the original green-painted door and the tall armoire used to store china. The pale, polished floor reflects natural light and the glow of the quirky, contemporary ceiling lights.

A traditional country kitchen is full of beguiling color, from the yellow walls and the faded flowers of the slipcover on the comfortable sofa to the brightly colored spongeware that crowds the shelves of the dresser and the modern still life propped above it.

OPPOSITE **The dining area of this London basement takes a thoroughly modern approach to entertaining within a reassuringly familiar context. Colored plastic chairs surround the circular table. White china—sculptural vases and "broken" plates on the wall—contrasts with the prevailing greenness.**

candlesticks—not to mention the flowers—are nowadays considerably simpler. All inject fresh, pretty color into any kitchen or dining area. In yesterday's dining rooms, paintings covered the deep-colored walls. Kitchen eating may mean you have less room for pictures—wall space is quickly covered with cabinets—but remember that even one picture provides a

THIS PAGE **City basements can be dark and dank. Here, the rich tones of old flagstones inspired a simple scheme in two shades of green. Walls are lined with tongue and groove and the cupboards have similar painted plank doors. The soft aqueous colors complement a modern metal range stove and sleek metal refrigerator, as well as the arrangement of pans and the metal vegetable stand. Each of these elements reflects light to different degrees, animating the simple-seeming scheme. A row of bright recipe books and a small antique pine cupboard used for glasses prevent the room appearing monotonous.**

The informality that is central to kitchen eating will influence the furniture you include in this room. Cooking often involves periods of waiting; provide a comfortable armchair or sofa for the cook. This will also add to the room's feeling of being lived in, which is in itself welcoming and relaxing. In a determinedly neutral kitchen or dining room, a handsomely covered chair can contribute a shot of positive color. You may wish to choose furniture that has a friendly, unprecious look, appropriate to the constant use to which kitchens are put. This contrasts with the smarter, more formal furniture associated with dining rooms. If you have fitted kitchen cabinets, their color will influence the decisions you make about freestanding furniture. Unfitted kitchens allow a greater degree of flexibility because they are less permanent and cheaper to alter. They also make greater demands on you at the planning stage, since unfitted kitchens make less efficient use of space and will require more dexterity if you are to accommodate tidily all the storage, appliances, and surfaces you need.

It is true that fabric absorbs food smells, one reason why kitchens have traditionally had simple window treatments. A separate dining room allows you to decorate more traditionally, using curtains and chair covers to add color and pattern. But it *is* possible to use fabric in a kitchen. Restrict yourself to shades or make a

talking point and an alternative focus, drawing attention away from the cook. As in any room, the right picture can inspire a whole scheme. Remember to plan your decorating so that the picture which provided the starting point is not lost in the details that accrue afterwards.

The only color in this large modern kitchen comes from the natural elements: the polished pine floorboards, the molded seats of the butterfly chairs, the wooden counters—and the cooking ingredients. A wall of charcoal tiles (reflected in the surface of the table) creates a sense of intimacy at night for grown-up entertaining.

This formal dining room plays witty games with historic decorating conventions. Instead of being hung with damask or patterned woven cloth, the walls are lined with a subtly three-dimensional grasscloth that contributes color and texture. Its neutral colors are reflected throughout the room, in which a soft raspberry carpet is laid over glossy black floorboards. Nothing detracts from the view.

OPPOSITE **The traditionally built kitchen cabinets here recall old-fashioned pantries. Yellow walls complement powder-blue cupboards. Unpainted cupboard knobs and the leather-covered radio provide darker accents.**

THIS PAGE **This dining room feels more like a home office or study, which increases its versatility. The colors are predominantly neutral—in contrast to traditional dining rooms—with bold accents, such as the green chairs. Unobtrusive calico shades provide privacy at night. This is a room in which china, glass, food, flowers, candles, and the guests themselves provide the principal notes of color.**

sumptuous cloth for your table, which can be removed for everyday living. Cover dining room chairs, an armchair, even bar stools in your favorite fabric, and echo its colors in china or lampshades. Remember, though, that simplicity can be hard to maintain in a room in which you store, prepare, and eat food: you may not want the added distraction of a busy or very vibrant fabric. Leave visual space for food to speak for itself—and enjoy cooking it and sharing it with family and friends.

no-color color

We all know that cooking demands hygiene. This partly accounts for the popularity in kitchens of pale colors and the wipe-clean neutrality of metallic surfaces. But food is by nature bright and colorful. Kitchens attract color even if we seek to banish it. It is possible to give in to this impulse and retain an essentially neutral kitchen that is nevertheless enlivened by shots of bright color. Arrange a dozen limes in a clear glass fruit bowl, fill a vase with oranges and lemons, store pasta, brown rice, coffee, and cane sugar in clear containers. Cover your table with a pretty cloth, or bind a pale shade with bright ribbon. Choose hand towels and dishtowels with a single stripe of color, or stand on the window sill a simple zinc planter filled with basil, parsley, oregano, and mint. Grow edible flowers in a hand-thrown pot. Paint open shelving to contrast with pale walls, and let your glasses and china sing out. Paint or line with wallpaper the insides of glass-fronted cupboards. Lay a smart, modern floor of rubber tiles or updated linoleum, and lay your table with bright place mats in complementary colors. Use colored enamel pans or hang a vintage colander, sugar shaker, and flour dredger from under-cupboard hooks. Each adds a note of color that, vibrant in itself, highlights positively the prevailing paleness.

THIS PAGE **Both these kitchens are completely white. Color is introduced through furniture, seat pads, decorative accessories such as the scarlet-lined bowl, a handsome rug, pictures on the wall, and simple but effective piles of fruit in glass vases. Against the white background, notes of color sing out. Color prevents the rooms from appearing clinical or sterile.**

OPPOSITE **A set of twelve boldly framed antique pictures made of pressed and dried leaves and flowers forms an arresting decorative statement in this creamy traditional kitchen in London. In their black frames, the pictures create an instant focal point. They break up the pale expanse, defining the space and injecting an element of drama. In the same way, the wooden counter contrasts with painted cabinets.**

sleeping with color

Your bedroom is your haven from the world, a personal sanctuary whether you share it or occupy it alone. In confined or open-plan spaces, you may wish to decorate your bedroom to blend harmoniously with the remainder of the house or apartment but, appropriately in a room for dreaming, this is also somewhere you can make dreams reality.

A bedroom is the ultimate sanctum, the one room in the house which no one else need see. This is the room in which to take refuge when the mood seizes you—like Garbo, alone.

As elsewhere, you will need to think at the outset about quantities of light and the volume of space. There is one important additional caveat to consider at the mood-board stage: are you a morning or an evening person? Do you really want to pry open your eyes to find yourself surrounded by vivid green walls, or is the scheme that makes you feel glamorous and special at night, lit by softly shaded lamps, all too much in the bright light of day after working late the previous evening? However much you long for a room that is dramatic, arresting, or uber-chic, don't overlook your more basic needs for relaxation, comfort, and freshness.

OPPOSITE **Colored bedlinen, colored walls, and large-scale paintings make this a bold, bright bedroom. It is prevented from becoming overwhelming by the simple white shade, the use of white-painted architectural elements to balance the yellow wall color and the simple styling of the bed, with its plain upholstered divan and headboard.**

ABOVE **The colors of this handsome bedroom are inspired by the painting above the bed. The painting's pairing of charcoal and old gold has been translated into a considered scheme of yellow and black. Neutral elements such as the glass lamps with their white shades vary the pace, as do the bold animal-print patterns.**

sleeping with color

Like living rooms, with their inevitable accumulation of magazines, newspapers, and books, family photographs, flowers, or plants, bedrooms present the problem that there can be too much color around. A dressing table covered in perfume bottles and cosmetics, clothes abandoned temporarily over the back of a chair, books heaped on a bedside table, cushions piled against a headboard, the pretty pattern of a quilt or bedcover, postcards tucked into the frame of a mirror or picture, all add extraneous color notes to what can easily become a busy room. A well-decorated bedroom needs planning and organization: you need storage even where space is at a premium, and plenty of it. And you need to banish the clutter at least at the beginning—that will come later! Keep at the back of your mind the mélange of colors that will intrude by accident throughout the planning stage of your bedroom's decoration, and choose either something bold that carries all before it, drawing attention away from the clutter, or something gentle and accommodating that will act as a harmonious foil to the many color accents. The recent trend for vintage-inspired, shabby-chic decorating works particularly well in bedrooms, especially girls' rooms. But for so many colors and patterns to work together well demands organization and a surprising amount of

This sophisticated scheme uses a number of colors with a deft touch. The walls have been lined with an irregular patchwork of torn leather fragments in caramel and toffee shades—a warm foil for the studded, white leather-upholstered bed, green glass mirror frame, mottled green **glass lamp, and rich teal curtains. Within this palette, contrasting patterns add vigor—an antique nursing chair covered in a pretty floral fabric, zebra-print cushions, and a pair of herringbone check cushions. The effect is relaxing and stylish, and equally appropriate for a man or a woman.**

Both these bedrooms have been painted yellow. In this bedroom a number of different shades create a bright, cozy cocoon full of year-round, day-long sunshine. In the room opposite, yellow walls provide a soft background for red-painted furniture and timeless floral fabrics.

discipline. Hold on to a firm image of how you want the finished room to look.

When it comes to deciding on the style of a bedroom, the most important question is who will be sleeping there? A girl about town who wants a classically pretty but of-the-moment bedroom can update floral chintziness by using color in place of pattern. Opt for a simply shaped headboard upholstered in a strong, stark color or something kitsch and sugary. Choose your fabric carefully. Suede, leather, ponyskin, velvet, and chenille all look luxurious and provide a simple backdrop for cushions or pillows, whether you choose crisp white bedlinen for contrast or pretty cushions piled on top of an antique quilt. To avoid pattern altogether while still maintaining interest, layer different shades of the same color, or choose a selection of complementary colors from the color wheel and use them to create a stylish cocktail. If your bed has a headboard, consider whether you want to repeat this color note in curtains or a dust ruffle. In this case, choose contrasting colors for the walls and any upholstered furniture in order to prevent the room from appearing too orderly. Too much of the same or too rigid an insistence on a very restricted palette can appear monotonous, soulless, or impersonal.

As in other rooms of the home, identify how you intend to use the room. Is this simply

a space for sleeping or do you write letters, read, listen to music, watch television, or have breakfast or supper in your bedroom? Does the room have an adjoining bathroom and will whatever scheme you decide on need to work there, too? Are you lucky enough to have a dressing room that accommodates all your clothes? In the case of a child's bedroom, is the room also somewhere the child plays on rainy days, does homework, or watches DVDs with a friend?

There is a theory that more than half the world's population would choose blue as their

In both these red bedrooms, the use of white counterbalances the effect of this potentially unrelaxing color. Here, pine floorboards and a white-ground comforter contrast with deep maroon. Opposite, in a large-scale damask-pattern wallpaper, the white motif softens the ruby background. A bright, overscaled pendant light adds a note of fun.

THIS PAGE **Bright blue walls and bold green carpet suggest a summer sky above rolling lawns. By stimulating memories of idyllic childhood summers, this is a positive, "happy" combination of colors.**

OPPOSITE **In this stylish modern bedroom, color is introduced at floor level: the white bed "floats" on a shimmering "pool" of glossy blue resin. Reflective surfaces maximize light and color. White linen and rich woody tones balance the bold floor color, emphasizing the textural element of this chic, sleek scheme.**

favorite color. Blue, the color of the sky, the sea, duck eggs, periwinkles, and delphiniums. It makes sense that blue is so often first choice for decorating bedrooms as well. A bright summer sky lifts our spirits. The classic combination of blue and white suggests clouds scudding across the sky, old English willow pattern (England's best-known china), Delft, or Oriental porcelain, the freshness of gingham.

Blue and white is a useful starting point for a bedroom, since it can be used successfully with accents of contrasting color, snatches of brown for a more chic look, red notes for extra warmth. Balance the summeriness of a blue and white bedroom with a chocolate-colored fur throw, or use blue and white elements in a boldly colored room for freshness and light—a blue-and-white throw over a chair or the foot of the bed in a room of strong green or yellow.

Since most of us work, we spend the majority of our time in our bedrooms at night, when there is little or no natural light from outdoors. Whatever color, texture, and pattern we choose for our bedroom's decoration, they need to look good in artificial light; ideally, in a bedroom, soft artificial light. Gentle, unassertive colors are very effective in these circumstances. Why not take your inspiration from the outdoors, where the only jarring notes are manmade?

THIS PAGE **Both these bedrooms update blue-and-white color combinations but do so without recourse to pattern, balancing painted elements, colored furniture, and accessories. Using several shades of blue, or adding new colors, prevents the rooms from looking chilly.**

OPPOSITE **In this comfortable bedroom in a house in the English countryside, walls the warm blue of summer sea and sky are the starting point for a traditional scheme that includes a number of decorative elements. Oriental plates nod towards the ever-popular willow pattern and framed bird pictures suggest the garden.**

Green walls remind us of nature's verdant gift, yellow is pretty and spring-like, a positive boon on those hard-to-get-out-of-bed mornings. The soft pink of the lining of a shell or the inside of rabbits' ears creates a tranquil, restful environment. Against a subtle backdrop of this sort, brighter or richer notes can be added with bedside lamps, which are essential, throws or the fabrics you choose. An antique or very expensive fabric can be

The starting point for this modern classical bedroom is the color-drenched painting of partygoers among classical ruins, which forms the room's focal point. The colors of the bright foliage in the picture inspired the rich amethyst cover of the armchair. Accessories complement the painting without drawing attention from it.

used in small quantities to make a curtain around a dressing table or to cover the seat of a little chair. The result is a note of luxury and individuality, and a shot of your favorite color that is easily incorporated within the wider scheme. Just work everything else around it. In the same way, if you like to read or watch television in bed, the wall opposite the bed is an obvious place to hang a favorite picture.

Choice of color marks these traditional bedrooms as masculine (RIGHT) **and feminine** (BELOW)**. In both, white elements provide the blank canvas onto which color is projected. The white background of the large-scale floral wallpaper below prevents it from overwhelming the room, while the rich colors of the painting and blanket, right, are softened by pale walls, white woodwork, and floor.**

Alternatively, since the bed provides the focal point of any bedroom, the wall behind the headboard may be your chosen spot for hanging pictures. Remember that pictures bring to a room colors of their own, and that a picture can appear to advantage or disadvantage depending upon the nature of its immediate surroundings. An exuberantly colorful lithograph by Matisse will hold its own against any backdrop, but a softly colored Victorian watercolor can easily be overwhelmed.

Bedrooms in which the storage is fitted can be almost empty of furniture. This allows the floor to take on a more prominent decorative role. If you have floorboards, carpet, or matting in a neutral palette, add interest with a rug. A bold, bright, modern rug makes it a joy to get out of bed, injecting vivid color into the room and enveloping your feet in softness. By contrast, a traditional fluffy sheepkskin or goatskin rug keeps bare feet warm in winter and cool in summer, and its pale colors usefully lighten a dark room. Remember that unless your intention is to create a deliberately busy space and to layer patterns and effects, a boldly patterned rug should be balanced by plainer elements. Use a rug as your starting point, picking out the principal colors in lampshades and decorative objects.

A bedroom needs to be warm to be inviting. If you have radiators, you may wish to consider covering them in many of your rooms, but it is often a good idea to leave those in your bedroom uncovered. This means that you can warm your nightclothes or indeed your daytime clothes on them on winter evenings and chilly mornings. It does not mean that you necessarily want to notice your radiators. The simplest way of making them recede into the wall is to paint the whole radiator the same color as the walls.

Choose fabric carefully. Suede, leather, ponyskin, velvet, and chenille all provide a simple backdrop for cushions or pillows, whether you choose crisp white bedlinen for contrast or pretty cushions piled on top of an antique quilt.

In bedrooms shared by a couple, color can be used to prevent the bedroom appearing overtly feminine. Brown, gray, or blue, for example, create an atmosphere that is masculine, modern, and chic. Partner brown curtains or walls with white woodwork and leather-covered folding tables or lamps for a contemporary look that has a feeling of tactile richness. Use "male" fabrics such as tweed, plaid, and corduroy, cover a chair in men's suiting fabric, and avoid fussy lamps. The effect can be as rural or metropolitan as you like.

You can also do this with wardrobes and closets. The result is a more intense burst of color in the room, but making the space appear less cluttered and more coherent since it reads as a single, same-color entity. This serves additionally to make it more visually relaxing, a calmer room in which to unwind and sleep.

This very disciplined room is decorated in a small number of close colors. Accents of black and white break up the space, keeping the look personal and interesting.

no-color color

A comfortable bed with crisp white bedlinen is the ultimate luxury. Since white remains our favorite color for bedlinen, it is a short hop to deciding to decorate the whole bedroom in a neutral palette. But what can look beguilingly clean and fresh can also appear clinical and sterile.

A wall of family photographs reprinted as black-and-white images all the same size, and simply, uniformly framed injects personality and an extra color note. Perhaps their silvery or sepia shadows will inspire accessories in recessive tertiary shades. Alternatively, opt for notes of bright color to emphasize by contrast the paleness of the surrounding space: scarlet lampshades, or a colorful rug or throw. Trim neutral curtains or shades with bold edging and place bright cushions on a snowy bed. Choose two colors (used carefully they will enhance, not destroy, the impact of the neutral background)—a pink cashmere bedcover with chocolate felt cushions or a rough-woven peppermint linen dust ruffle. Introduce color in a bright frame for a mirror or hang bold prints in deep, white-painted frames. Paint a wooden floor a checkerboard of blue and white diamonds or hang colored glass droplets from a modern chandelier. For maximum impact, hang a favorite piece of bright clothing against a completely white wall or paint radiators stark, matt black like modern sculptural installations.

OPPOSITE **Glamorous silver wallpaper makes a dramatic statement here. The paper and Venetian-style mirror hung against it reflect the changing colors of light through the day and the room's inhabitants, who contribute living color to the metallic monochrome scheme.**

RIGHT **In this unfussy room, a color-free background focuses attention on the bed—the natural focal point of a bedroom —with its colored bedlinen. White shelves throw into relief book spines and colored glass vases. Two-tone bedside units add a quirky color note.**

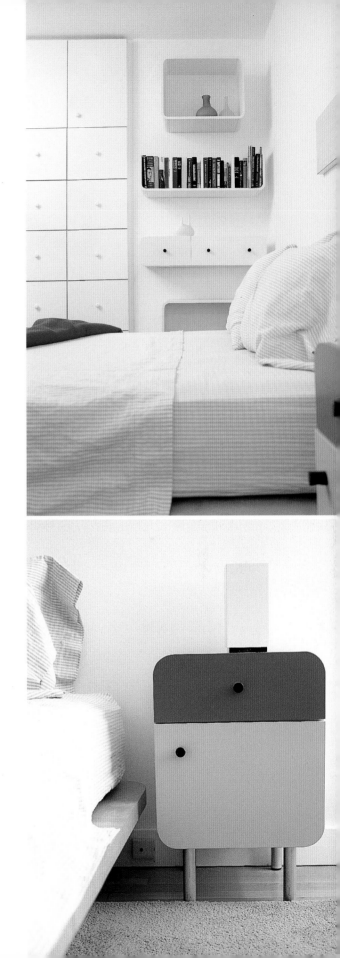

WAYS YIELD TO
EMPTATION
CAUSE IT MAY
NOT PASS
UR WAY AGAIN

These bedrooms make extensive use of black which, handled carefully, can create a safe embrace remote from the world outside. In the bedroom opposite, the lustrous sheen of the velvet cushions, the glossy patina of the closet doors, the bright photograph, and the pale carpet counter the darkness. In this New York bedroom decorated in black, white, and silver, interest is provided by the juxtaposition of the contrasting shades.

private color

THIS PAGE **This simple bathroom is decorated in an appropriately aqueous shade of pale Nile green, the wall color matching the small mosaic tiles used for the side of the tub. A deep white backsplash provides contrast and echoes the white of the tub itself. The stark outline of a stalking trophy makes a dramatic decorative statement. The backsplash incorporates a recessed shelf for bath products, allowing them to be openly but tidily displayed, while remaining close at hand for the bather.**

OPPOSITE **This modern bathroom in a Victorian house offers a contemporary take on decorating with tiles. A refreshing palette of blue and green suggests cleanliness and freshness, as well as fostering a tranquil atmosphere that is augmented by the simplicity and lack of clutter in the room.**

If your home has more than one bathroom, try to designate one a public space for guests, and another a private space for your own use. This is the room in which to enjoy your favorite colors—with a single proviso. Remember that you use the bathroom early in the morning and late at night, in summer and winter, when you're tired and occasionally when you're ill.

Don't choose a color that you know will compound a headache or discourage you from relaxing in a lazy bath. Bear in mind that though the ideal bathroom provides subdued lighting at night, it needs effective task lighting at other times, for makeup or shaving. The color choices you make in your bathroom will influence the room's lighting requirements.

ABOVE **Modern tiles are available in myriad colors, sizes, and materials. Where more than one color is used, small, mosaic-style tiles create a more understated look than their larger counterparts. In this bathroom, mosaic tiles in three shades of blue combine with an orange sliding door.**

THIS PICTURE **Tiles are a practical, good-looking design solution for any bathroom, with their resistance to condensation. Used as an all-over wall treatment, they create a simple background for bathing.**

private color

In this dramatic bathroom, the paint used for the walls was color matched to the modern mosaic tiles which cover the floor and the sides of the sink and tub. The effect is both visually arresting and gentle. The choice of lavender, with its soothing associations, makes for a tranquil space in which it is relaxing to spend time at any point in the day. The lavender background serves to intensify the whiteness of the sink and tub, creating a look that is clean but not sterile. The polished chrome faucets and shower and the unframed mirror harmonize with and reflect the surrounding color.

Darker colors may need to be balanced by areas of white and clever use of mirror, both of which also increase the sense of space (useful in what is often a small room). Make bathroom equipment white—avoid colored tubs, sinks, or toilets. This will provide a counterpoint to colored decorating, as will the metallic surfaces of faucets and showerheads.

Your private bathroom is where you will want to sink into a tub after a long day at work or to prepare for a party. White fixtures provide a crisp, fresh look and create a clean counterfoil to your chosen colors, while modern circular sinks in stone or glass are sufficiently neutral to fit any scheme. Not all colored fixtures are taboo: a reconditioned 19th-century copper bathtub glitters and gleams, inviting you to decorate around it.

Bathrooms currently tend towards the very modern or the consciously nostalgic. Don't automatically decide that this is a fabric-free zone. Since part of the room's purpose is to provide somewhere for relaxing, apply the criteria used in your living room. Be inspired by a swatch of vintage fabric—make it into curtains, a shower curtain, or a cushion for an armchair beside the bath. A chair near the bathtub or shower gives you a place to put your clothes while you wash, while a small table similarly placed provides a resting place for a drink or book. Painted furniture is useful in a bathroom, where steam and condensation can rob highly polished furniture of its gloss. A pretty chair and a painted bathside table are both ways of bringing color to the room. You may wish to construct your mood board around that furniture, around the swatch of vintage fabric, or an antique tile you have found. Alternatively, these elements can provide points of contrast with the sleek functionality of the bathroom fixtures.

As with any room, consider the purpose and comfort of the room and the atmosphere you wish it to evoke. Do you love the

ABOVE **Crimson, high-gloss, small mosaic tiles create instant modern drama. Elements of white soften the effect without enervating the boldness of the scheme.**

OPPOSITE **A single large window lightens the effect of this rich tomato-red bathroom with a slate floor. A frosted-glass door and chrome towel rail add additional color notes, while reflecting light into the room.**

streamlined luxury of boutique hotels? Do pale neutrals or shiny white remind you of relaxing spas? Do you crave the cocooning of rich chocolate-painted walls? Do you want a look that is crisply tailored or softer and more haphazard; a feminine haven of pink and powder blue, or the shimmering surfaces and sinuous lines of Hollywood glamour? Will it be a country house-style bathroom, with chintz-covered chairs and curtains or tongue and groove, sufficiently tough for family life?

The modern bathroom is not only more comfortable but also more sophisticated than its predecessor. Tiles no longer recall public restrooms. Colorful glass mosaic tiles in aqueous hues provide a background of color for lining walls, the floor, and the shower. Metallic luster tiles in gold and bronze hint at Byzantine opulence, encouraging the weary bather to lie back and dream.

If your bathtub is not freestanding, it will need a panel around it. This can be painted the same color as the walls and any other fitted furniture, such as

Citrus colors suggest heat, vacations, and the sun. They also serve as a wake-up call on sluggish winter mornings. In both these bathrooms— one yellow, the other orange— strong color complements and enhances the use of white and neutral shades. When decorating with such a vivid backdrop, it is essential to provide adequate storage to clear away miscellaneous color notes in the form of bathroom products and lotions.

ABOVE **Only one wall of this bathroom has been painted strong yellow. The combination of the yellow wall, the vibrant abstract painting, and the matching yellow case used as a bathroom cabinet creates an appearance of brightness that is cheerful and uplifting.**

LEFT **This stunning washroom is unashamedly colorful and invigorating, with its tessellation of vivid colors painted onto the walls like tiles. The pale lower wall prevents the impact overwhelming the viewer.**

The starting point for this glamorous, large London bathroom was the magnificent reconditioned 19th-century copper tub positioned centrally: it glows with light and color. Color-washed pale sienna walls echo its luster in more subdued form, while a shimmering wall of gold leaf, lit with spots, is unashamedly opulent, alive with light and color. Floor-to-ceiling windows hung with filmy muslin curtains provide privacy without excluding light.

bathroom cabinets. Choosing an intense, warm color such as eggplant purple or the uncompromising inkiness of black or midnight blue is one way of introducing drama and creating a masculine atmosphere in a potentially feminine room.

Restricting bathroom fixtures to white makes walls and floors the obvious way of introducing color to the room. If your bathroom is next door to a bedroom or attached to it, consider

66 Choosing an intense color such as eggplant purple or the uncompromising inkiness of black or midnight blue introduces drama. 99

This attic bathroom has only one small window above the tub. Leaving it uncurtained and painting the ceiling above it and the sloping walls white maximizes natural light as well as providing a contrast with the dark-painted tongue-and-groove paneling. A painted Victorian washstand adds a lighter color accent, echoed in the pitcher on the bathtub.

the effect of your chosen color when the connecting door is open. Such intimate spaces should flow into one another seamlessly with no jarring notes. This could be a reason for using the same color in both, especially if your choice is bold. Alternatively, a private bathroom could be the place to use a favorite color you have used successfully elsewhere in the house. In small houses or apartments, this adds to a feeling of overall coherence. There is no reason not to use wallpaper in the bathroom if this is your preferred option for introducing color and interest. Use Plexiglas panels over the wallpaper closest to the tub and sink to prevent water damage and to avoid the need for tiles.

Because bathrooms invariably contain a limited amount of furniture, flooring is more exposed than in many rooms and acquires greater significance. Again,

This guest bathroom is visible from the bedroom it serves, and decorated in shades of warm taupe that harmonize with the neutral bedroom. The room has an almost Zen-like simplicity. The central tub is deliberately the focal point, positioned to be fully visible from the bedroom. The sides of the tub are painted deep, rich brown. The bathtub faucets are centrally mounted below a single picture. The simple sink stands out of sight.

This smart modern bathroom opens off a sleek dressing room. The same marble mosaic tiles have been laid on the floor and in the shower tray. Drawing the eye towards the trio of bright windows, colors in the room become lighter from floor to ceiling. The walls are partly tiled in pale buff and painted white above. Glass shower doors with an invisible frame contribute to the impression of lightness.

you will need to consider if you want to go dark or light. Black slate makes a dramatic contribution to a color scheme, in stark contrast to white fixtures, and is also easy to maintain. Limestone is useful in a neutral scheme, as is its costlier cousin marble. All can be laid over underfloor heating systems, so that the room not only looks good but feels good too. Stone and marble tiles can also be used to line walls or the side of the tub for an all-over color effect.

If you are fortunate enough to have a wooden floor in your bathroom, you may want to paint the boards. Durable floor paints are now available in many colors, but white and off-white shades, with their suggestion of Scandinavian style, remain the most popular. Pale, fresh, painted floors not only lighten a small room

Every surface of this country bathroom has been painted. The walls are partly lined with painted tongue and groove boards, which also encase the bathtub. A chintz-covered armchair is comfortable and colorful. A collection of antique china plates injects color, pattern, and prettiness.

but also make the ceiling appear higher, further increasing the sense of space. A neutral floor also leaves your options open for deeper, brighter wall colors.

With their view of sky and trees, tall buildings or distant hills, windows admit color to any room. In many bathrooms, a window is an obvious focal point. Think about how to treat it decoratively. A window in a bathroom that is not overlooked may not need any treatment: simply paint the frame your preferred color and think of it as a picture frame flooding the room with light. In other circumstances, a shade may work better than curtains; or you may choose shutters, which are sleek and echo the tailored look of bathroom cabinetry. Wooden shutters can be painted to match other wooden elements, adding to the effect of coherence and visual balance. This helps make your bathroom relaxing by consolidating its pared-down appearance, eliminating distractions. Remember that, above all, bathrooms need to *work*—and to feel pampering, clean, and fresh.

ABOVE LEFT **In this off-white bathroom, the impedimenta that accumulate in a bathroom contribute the color necessary to enliven the small space: a smart dressing gown hung on the back of the door; books piled on a chair; a painting above the door.**

ABOVE RIGHT **Though neutral, this paneled bathroom has a warm atmosphere—partly the result of the soft, pale honey color of the walls, partly the impact of the wooden floor.**

private color

A limestone sink shelf, bathtub, and floor, and white walls create a peaceful atmosphere in this large, top-lit bathroom. Wicker storage cases, a basket of plump natural sponges, and the polished darkwood frames of the tall mirror and bathside stool inject color, personalizing a handsome room.

RIGHT **Tertiary-colored mosaic tiles provide a neutral background in this bathroom, in which light reflected off smooth metallic doors provides shifting notes of color.**

BELOW **The walls of this bathroom have been lined with unpolished slate tiles. The stone has a strong color that changes during the course of the day, from warm purple in the midday sun to inky black at night. Pale pine shelves act as a counterpoint.**

no-color color

In the West, white is associated with cleanliness, and white or off-white bathrooms remain many people's preferred option. White surfaces bounce light back into the room from windows, mirrors, and artificial sources. White successfully partners the chrome and brushed nickel of many bathroom fixtures, and flatters the shimmer of mirror glass. If you want your bathroom to remain predominantly white, introduce color through accessories: a bowl of pale green olive-oil soaps, a blue glass bottle filled with bath oil, colored glass or china knobs on a cabinet, a picture hung above the bathtub, modern ceramics arranged like an abstract sculpture around the sides of the bath. Colored towels have the practical benefit of marking less easily with makeup than their white equivalents.

Traditionally watery colors such as blue and green share many positive, healing associations with white. Both blue and white and green and white are reliably crisp, fresh combinations that will not overwhelm an "uncolored" space. A tried-and-tested option is white walls and bathroom fixtures, with color added in curtains or shades. The beauty of this is that it leaves you free to use your favorite material, whatever its color, as it will be balanced by the white interior. Woven Portuguese bathmats in blue and white or red and white achieve a similar end; use a flowery rug to warm wooden floors, or cover a chair in crisp striped linen. As long as the background color of the rug and the fabric is neutral, the effect will not be overpowering.

White surfaces bounce light into the room from windows and mirrors. White partners the chrome and nickel of bathroom fixtures, and flatters the shimmer of mirror glass.

ABOVE **Even the soap is black in this dramatic bathroom. A circular mirror has been hung against a black-painted panel. It echoes the swirling motifs of the black-and-white shower curtain. White tiles, wall lights, and sink keep the look light; the unusual choice of black banishes any suggestion of a hospital bathroom.**

OPPOSITE **In this bathroom in which walls, floor, and ceiling are all black, the light-reflecting qualities of the surfaces are all-important. The walls have a subtle, lustrous sheen that reflects the light from the large window and the triple mirror-paneled bathroom cabinet. A simple white square sink and toilet provide contrast.**

resources

The Color Wheel Company
P. O. Box 130
Philomath, OR 97370
541-929-7526

www.colorwheelco.com
Color wheels to help you match tints, tones, and shades.

GENERAL RETAILERS

ABC Carpet & Home
888 Broadway
New York, NY 10003
212-473-3000

www.abchome.com

Bed, Bath & Beyond
620 Avenue of the Americas
New York, NY 10011
212-255-3550

www.bedbathandbeyond.com

Crate & Barrel
646 North Michigan Avenue
Chicago, IL 60611
312-787-5900

www.crateandbarrel.com

Home Depot
Check your telephone
directory for stores or visit

www.homedepot.com

IKEA
1800 E. McConnor Parkway
Schaumburg, IL 60173
847-969-9700

www.ikea.com

Pier One Imports
71 Fifth Avenue
New York, NY 10003
212-206-1911

www.pier1.com

Pottery Barn
600 Broadway
New York, NY 10012
212-219-2420

www.potterybarn.com

Restoration Hardware
935 Broadway
New York, NY 10010
212-260-9479

www.restorationhardware.com

The Terence Conran Shop
Bridgemarket
407 East 59th Street
New York, NY 10022
212-755-9079

www.conran.com

PAINT

Benjamin Moore Paints
51 Chestnut Ridge Road
Montvale, NJ 07645
800-334-0400

www.benjaminmooore.com
Over 1,400 colors, including historic styles.

Décor Color
2820 T.O. Boulevard
Thousand Oaks, CA 91362
805-495-7097

www.decorcolor.com
Range of unique and difficult-to-find paint products. Holds faux finishing classes.

Factory Paint and Decorating
55 Washington Street
Pembroke, MA 02358
800-696-3400

www.factorypaint.com
Wall coverings and paint.

Farrow & Ball
845-369-4912

www.farrow-ball.com
Historic paints.

Gracious Home
1220 Third Avenue
New York, NY 10021
212-517-6300

www.gracioushome.com
Hardware, paints, varnishes.

Krylon
800-4KRYLON

www.krylon.com

General-purpose paints, enamels, and latex; specialty paints; crackle paints, stone effects.

Old Fashioned Milk Paint Co.
436 Main Street
Groton, MA 01450
978-448-6336 for
distributors and mail order

www.milkpaint.com
Authentic milk-paint powders—add water and mix. They supply instructions and photos and also sell a milk-paint remover.

Pratt & Lambert Paints
800-BUY-PRATT

www.prattandlambert.com
Accolade paint products; flat, satin, enamel, and distinctive faux finishes.

Ralph Lauren Paint Collection
At Ralph Lauren
867 Madison Avenue
New York, NY 10021
212-606-2100
Call 800-379-POLO for other stockists of paint products

www.rlhome.polo.com
Signature collection of colors grouped in palettes.

FABRIC

Calico Fabric Quilt Shop
10 West Street
West Hatfield, MA 01088
866-247-9989

www.calicofabric.com
Over 3,000 bolts of fabric.

Duralee
1775 Fifth Avenue
Bay Shore, NY 11706
631-273-8800

www.duralee.com
Known for traditional designs in fashionable colorations.

Fabrics To Dye For
1 Charlestown Beach Road
Charlestown, RI 02813
888-322-1319

www.fabricstodyefor.com
Hand-painted fabrics, dyes, and kits; also available from various retail outlets.

Hancock Fabrics
1 Fashion Way
Baldwyn, MS 38824
877-FABRICS

www.hancockfabrics.com
Largest US fabric store; good for all basic decoration needs.

Laura Ashley
Call 803-396-7744 for
your nearest stockist.

www.lauraashley-usa.com
Floral, striped, checked, and solid cottons in many colors.

Lunn Fabrics Ltd.
317 East Main Street
Lancaster, OH 43130
740-654-2202

www.lunnfabrics.com
One-of-a-kind hand-dyed and painted fabrics in every color and design.

Reprodepot Fabrics
116 Pleasant Street
Easthampton, MA 01027
413-527-4047

www.reprodepotfabrics.com
Online store. Individually designed, vintage-inspired cotton fabrics in fun colors and designs.

Waverly

www.waverly.com
Online store. Decorative accessories including fabric, wallpaper, furniture, window treatments, tabletop, paint, and floor coverings.

index

Italics indicate captions.

PICTURE CREDITS

The publishers would like to thank all those who allowed us to photograph their homes for this book.

All photography by Chris Everard unless otherwise stated. Key: **ph**=photographer, **a**=above, **b**=below, **r**=right, **l**=left, **c**=center

Endpapers, 16–17, 50–53, 75, 96–97, 99–101, 127l Jamie Drake's Manhattan apartment; **1, 21a, 41–45, 47, 106** A London home designed by Naomi Cleaver; **2, 34–35, 82–83, 98, 127r** Fashion designer Catherine Malandrino's Manhattan apartment; **3, 8–9, 18–19, 48–49, 62–63, 81, 114** The Rug Company's Christopher and Suzanne Sharp's London home; **4, 10–11, 38–39, 110** Manhattan home of designer Matthew Patrick Smyth; **5–7, 32–33, 68–71** Tim and Celia Holman's house in London, designed by DIVE Architects Ltd; **12, 21b, 23, 46, 58, 64–65, 78–79, 84, 128–129** Simon and Coline Gillespie's home in North London; **13, 59, 76–77, 105** Davy Hezeman and Steven Pooters' home in Amsterdam; **14–15, 54, 111b, 120** Writer Rita Konig's house in London; **20, 40, 85, 109, 136** A family home in Norfolk; **22l** Philippe Model's apartment in Paris; **22r ph** Christopher Drake / Villa Marie, Ramatuelle, St Tropez; **24l ph** Christopher Drake / The home of Adrian and Belinda Hull in London, designed by architect Gus Alexander; **24r–25 ph** Fritz von der Schulenberg / Laura Bohn of LBDA; **26–27, 88–89, 113, 132–133, 141** Home of David Walsh, Creative Director of Inner Sanctum, London; **28l, 92** Chris Everard's cottage in Norfolk; **28r–29, 56–57, 95, 111a, 137l** Jeremy Hackett's house in London; **30–31, 66–67, 117, 140** Christopher Coleman's New York apartment; **36–37, 61a, 90–91, 134–135** New York family home designed by Shamir Shah; **55, 86–87, 93, 108l, 130–131, 137r** John Nicolson's house in Spitalfields, London; **60–61b, 72–73, 104, 107r inset, 121, 125** Tony Loizou of Pennington Robson—the Loizou's house in North London; **80** The London apartment of the Sheppard Day Design Partnership; **94a** An apartment in London designed by Jo Hagan of USE Architects; **94b** Interior designer Ann Boyd's own apartment in London; **102** Programmable House in London, designed by d-squared; **103** Fashion designer Carla Saibene's home in Milan; **107 background** Pemper and Rabiner home in New York, designed by David Khouri of Comma; **108r ph** Andrew Wood / Kurt Bredenbeck's apartment at the Barbican, London; **115** Mark Weinstein's apartment in New York designed by Lloyd Schwan; **116** Eric De Queker's apartment in Antwerp; **118–119** An actor's London home designed by Site Specific; **122al** Richard Oyarzabel's apartment in London designed by Jeff Kirkby of Urban Research Laboratory; **122b ph** Debi Treloar / Family home in Bankside, London designed by Dive Architects; **122ar, 123** Paul Brazier and Diane Lever's house in London designed by Carden & Cunietti; **124** A house in Highbury, London designed by Dale Loth Architects; **126l** An apartment in Paris designed by architects Fabienne Couvert and Guillaume Terver of cxt sarl d'architecture; **126r** Yuen-Wei Chew's apartment in London designed by Paul Daly Design Studio Ltd; **138** The Sugarman-Behun house on Long Island, New York; **139a** John Minshaw's former house in London designed by John Minshaw; **139b** Gomez/Murphy Loft in Hoxton, London designed by Urban Salon Ltd.

BUSINESS CREDITS

Ann Boyd Design Ltd *page 94b*
Studio 8, Fairbank Studios
Lots Road, London SW10 0NS
t. +44 20 7351 4098

Carden Cunietti *pages 122ar, 123*
81–83 Westbourne Park Road
London W2 5QH
t. +44 20 7229 8559
www.carden-cunietti.com

Carla Saibene (womenswear, accessories, and antiques) *page 103*
Via San Maurillio 20, Milan
t. +39 2 77 33 15 70

Catherine Malandrino
Fashion designer
pages 2, 34–35, 82–83, 98, 127r
www.catherinemalandrino.com

Christopher Coleman Interior Design
pages 30–31, 66–67, 117, 140
55 Washington Street, Suite 707
Brooklyn, NY 11021
t. 718 222 8984
www.ccinteriordesign.com

Comma (architecture, interiors, and furniture) *page 107 background*
131 Varick Street, Suite 1031
New York, NY 10013
t. 212 420 7866
www.comma-nyc.com

Fabienne Couvert, Guillaume Terver
cxt sarl d'architecture *page 126l*
12 Rue Saint Fiarcre, 75002 Paris
t. +33 1 55 34 98 50
www.couverterver-architectes.com

d-squared design *page 102*
t. +44 20 7253 2240

Dale Loth Architects *page 124*
1 Cliff Road, London NW1 9AJ
t. +44 20 7485 4003
www.dalelotharchitects.ltd.uk

DIVE Architects Ltd
pages 5–7, 32–33, 68–71, 122b
A009 The Jam Factory
19 Rothsay Street, London SE1 4UF
t. +44 20 7407 0955
www.divearchitects.com

Drake Design Associates
endpapers, 16–17, 50–53, 75, 96–97, 99–101, 127l
315 East 62nd Street
New York, NY 10021
t. 212 754 3099

Emma Bridgewater
pages 20, 40, 85, 109, 136
739 Fulham Road, London SW6 5UL
t. +44 20 7371 5489
www.emmabridgewater.co.uk

Eric De Queker *page 116*
Koninklijkelaan 44
2600 Berchem, Belgium
eric.de.queker@pandora.be

Steven Pooters, Co-owner Ganbaroo (marketing) *pages 13, 59, 76–77, 105*
Haarlemmerweg 317 L
1051 LG Amsterdam
t. +31 20 688 5818

Gus Alexander Architects *page 24l*
46–47 Britton Street
London EC1M 5NA
t. +44 20 7336 7227
www.gusalexanderarchitects.com

Inner Sanctum Interiors *pages 26–27, 88–89, 113, 132–133, 141*
32 Charlotte Road
London EC2A 3PB
t. +44 20 7613 3706
www.innersanctum.co.uk

John Minshaw Designs Ltd *page 139a*
17 Upper Wimpole Street
London W1H 6LU
t. +44 20 7258 5777
www.johnminshawdesigns.com

John Nicolson, Spitalfields, London
pages 55, 86–87, 93, 108l, 130–131, 137r
Available to hire as a location at
johnnynicolson@aol.com

Laura Bohn Design Associates
pages 24r–25
30 West 26th Street
New York, NY 10010
t. 212 645 3636 **www.lbda.com**

Lloyd Schwan Design *page 115*
New York, NY

Matthew Patrick Smyth Inc.
pages 4, 10–11, 38–39, 110
12 West 57th Street
New York, NY 10019
t. 212 333 5353
www.matthewsmyth.com

Naomi Cleaver Ltd
pages 1, 21a, 41–45, 47, 106
5 Sebastian Street
London EC1V 0HD
t. +44 20 7251 6990
www.naomicleaver.com

Paul Daly Design Studio Ltd
page 126r
Unit 7, 11 Hoxton Square
London N1 6NU
t. +44 20 7613 4855 **www.pauldaly.com**

Pennington Robson *pages 60–61b, 72–73, 104, 107r inset, 121, 125*
Tea Warehouse, 10A Lant Street
London SE1 1QR
t. +44 20 7378 0671
www.penningtonrobson.co.uk

Philippe Model (decoration, home furnishings, and coverings) *page 22l*
33 Place du Marché St Honoré
75001 Paris
t. +33 1 42 96 89 02

ROLLO Contemporary Art
pages 12, 21b, 23, 46, 58, 64–65, 78–79, 84, 128–129
17 Compton Terrace, London N1 2UN
t. +44 20 7493 8383 **www.rolloart.com**

Shamir Shah Design *pages 36–37, 61a, 90–91, 134–135*
10 Greene Street
New York, NY 10013
t. 212 274 7476
www.shamirshahdesign.com

Sheppard Day Design Partnership
page 80
t. +44 20 7821 2222

Site Specific Ltd *pages 118–119*
305 Curtain House
134–146 Curtain Road
London EC2A 3AR
t. +44 20 7689 3200
www.sitespecificltd.co.uk

Davy Hezemans, Co-owner Spice PR
pages 13, 59, 76–77, 105
Leidsegracht 38–40
1016 CM – Amsterdam
t. +31 65 530 0375

The Rug Company *pages 3, 8–9, 18–19, 48–49, 62–63, 81, 114*
124 Holland Park Avenue
London W11 4UE
t. +44 20 7229 5148
www.therugcompany.info

Jeff Kirby Urban Research Lab
page 122al
www.smcurbanlab.com

Urban Salon Ltd *page 139b*
Unit D, Flat Iron Yard, Ayres Street
London SE1 1ES
t. +44 20 7357 8800

USE Architects *page 94a*
Unit 12, 47–49 Tudor Road
London E9 7SN
t. +44 20 8986 8111
use.arch@virgin.net

Villa Marie, Ramatuelle *page 22r*
St Tropez, France
t. +33 4 94 97 40 22
www.c-h-m.com